EXIT

PREPARE TO SELL YOUR BUSINESS WITHOUT REGRET

RYAN GUTH

PERMISSION TO
EXIT

PREPARE TO SELL YOUR BUSINESS WITHOUT REGRET

Connor!
Thank you for being on the team! Only pull the chute if you know who packed it. :)

RYAN GUTH

Scripture taken from the NEW AMERICAN STANDARD BIBLE®, Copyright ©1960, 1962, 1963, 1971, 1972, 1973, 1975, 1977, 1995 by The Lockman Foundation. Used with permission.

Copyright 2024 © Goldfin Group

All rights reserved. No part of this book may be reproduced or transmitted in any form or by any means, electronic or mechanical, including photocopying, recording, or by any information storage and retrieval system without written permission of the publisher, except for the inclusion of brief quotations in a review.

Designed by Dino Marino, www.dinomarinodesign.com.

E-book ISBN: 979-8-9899715-1-0
Paperback ISBN: 979-8-9899715-0-3

The information provided in this text is general in nature, does not take into consideration the reader's personal circumstances, and is therefore not intended to be a substitute for specific, individualized financial, legal, and tax advice. For advice specific to your own personal circumstances, we suggest that you consult with qualified and properly licensed financial, legal, and/or tax professionals.

Tax laws and provisions are subject to change. The author, SCF Securities, Inc., and SCF Investment Advisors, Inc. do not offer tax or legal advice or services.

There is no assurance that the techniques and strategies mentioned are suitable for all individuals or will yield positive outcomes.

Finally, references to various websites, products, and companies are not an endorsement, but are merely provided as general information purposes.

Securities are offered through SCF Securities, Inc. Member FINRA & SIPC. Investment Advisory Services are offered through SCF Investment Advisors, Inc., an SEC Registered Investment Adviser. Ryan Guth is a registered representative of SCF Securities, Inc., and an investment advisor representative of SCF Investment Advisors, Inc. Goldfin Group and the SCF companies are not affiliated.

SPECIAL INVITATION

Be sure to sign up for instant access to all of the resources and bonuses included in this book:

Goldfin.Group/ExitBook

DEDICATION

This book is dedicated to my clients—those I've had the honor of serving in the past, those I work with today, and those I will meet in the future. My experiences with both the scarcity and abundance of wealth have deeply formed my understanding of its significant impact on our lives and dreams.

It's essential to understand that money is not inherently evil but is not a reliable guide either. True clarity comes from knowing yourself, your values, and your goals. Understanding these before wealth transforms your life can help you protect your relationships, inspire your children to greatness, and increase your ability to continue doing good in a world that needs you more than ever.

I believe that a combination of your unique talents, hard work, and a touch of divine providence has led you to where you are now.

Let's challenge each other to continue being responsible stewards and role models of these blessings. Thank you for embarking on this journey with me.

With gratitude,
Ryan Guth, December 2023

TABLE OF CONTENTS

INTRODUCTION..i

CHAPTER ONE
LAYING THE FOUNDATIONS
OF SUCCESS.. 1

CHAPTER TWO
ALIGNING FAMILY, VALUES,
AND MISSION..15

CHAPTER THREE
CRAFTING YOUR FINANCIAL BLUEPRINT...... 30

CHAPTER FOUR
INVESTING WITH A
LONG-TERM OUTLOOK...................................... 45

CHAPTER FIVE
SAFEGUARDING YOUR JOURNEY:
PROTECTION AND RISK MANAGEMENT 57

CHAPTER SIX
   BUILDING YOUR TEAM OF A-PLAYERS 74

CHAPTER SEVEN
   GRANTING YOURSELF
   PERMISSION TO EXIT 91

NOTHING BUT NEXT PODCAST........................... 97

APPENDIX: GOLDFIN GROUP SERVICES........... 98

PLEASE REVIEW THIS BOOK 100

GRATITUDE.. 101

WHO IS RYAN GUTH? 103

INTRODUCTION

Exit. The word conjures up all sorts of negative emotions.

It can make you feel like you're leaving something good behind. A character in a play must *exit stage left or right* after every scene. An actor giving an Oscar speech is shooed off stage with *exit music*. You can end a great company career with an anti-climactic *exit interview*.

The word can also give you a sense of anxiety. You're more likely to get into a car accident on an *exit ramp* than an entrance ramp. You can be subjected to an *exit poll* after voting in an election. Ask a citizen of the U.K. about a recent stressful time, and they might start talking about *Brexit*.

At its worst, *exit* represents something we hope to avoid. You don't want to get caught in a crowd during an emergency, which is why you should never *block the exit*. You definitely want to avoid getting shot, which might leave a terrible *exit wound* or perhaps even cause you to make a *final exit* from this life.

When it comes to exiting your business, it's less dramatic but can feel just as stressful. You might feel anxious that you're leaving behind something wonderful you've created. You also want to avoid the mistakes of leaving money on the table or exiting too early or too late.

As a wealth manager who specializes in working with successful entrepreneurs, many of whom are exiting their businesses, I've met more than a few people who feel anxious during this season of their careers. I also know firsthand what it feels like to build a great business—one giving me a ton of purpose and joy—and having to contemplate the intricacies of selling it while still enjoying the day-to-day, but wondering if it is a good time—or a good price.

Maybe you picked up this book because you wish to sell in the near future and want to minimize the possibility of regret. Selling your business isn't just a transaction. For many, it's the beginning of a new phase of life. It's also a major change to your family's economic engine. I'm here to help. When you finish *Permission to*

Exit, having completed the "Action Steps" at the end of each chapter, you'll hopefully come away with a newfound confidence and clarity to help you plan a successful exit and an exciting launch into your next adventure.

DO YOU KNOW STEVE?

Meet Steve, a character who may resonate with many entrepreneurs. At forty-one, he's navigated a decade of growing his business alongside his thirteen-year marriage and raising three children. Despite his apparent success, Steve's story reveals the challenges of balancing business with family life. His commitment to his business often overshadows time with loved ones, making him feel more like an employee rather than the leader of his company.

Steve's struggle is not just about the day-to-day demands but also the bigger picture: preparing for a successful exit from his business without regrets. He's caught in the cycle of constantly reacting to business needs, often at the expense of personal time and strategic planning.

Steve recognizes this imbalance. His faith, family, and friendships—his cornerstones—have often been relegated to second place. He keeps promising himself that he'll reset his priorities after reaching the next milestone. However, as the nature of entrepreneurship goes, these milestones keep shifting, and the goalposts keep moving further down the field. With every new achievement, Steve feels a mix of triumph and a pang of regret, realizing that each step forward in business is a step away from cherished moments with loved ones.

Steve's story is a common one, where the game of business is as much about what we gain as it is about what we risk leaving behind.

SUCCESSFUL BUT UNPREPARED

Despite his success, Steve is vulnerable to a less-than-ideal exit experience, a common scenario among entrepreneurs. This vulnerability stems from a lack of preparedness in three critical areas: business dependency, family financial security, and readiness for a significant financial windfall. Entrepreneurs like Steve often have their net worth tied up in their businesses, making strategic planning for an exit crucial.

Consider this: If you had to disconnect completely for two months, what would happen to your business? This thought often unsettles entrepreneurs because it highlights a dual dependence: the business's reliance on them and, more crucially, their personal reliance on the business. The latter can be particularly daunting as it reflects a deeper, more personal vulnerability.

Now, imagine if you weren't there to join your family for breakfast tomorrow. How would this affect them financially? This question cuts to the core of your responsibilities, extending beyond your business to the well-being of your family. It underscores the importance of preparing not just for the continuity of your business, but also for the long-term financial security of your loved ones.

Finally, envision receiving a wire transfer tomorrow for your ideal selling price. How prepared are you to manage this influx of wealth? Think about your readiness in terms of tax planning, estate management, investment strategies, and aligning these with your personal goals and values. If your readiness score is below eight out of ten, it's time to reflect. As a business owner, with the majority of your net worth likely tied up in your business, traditional financial assets like a 401(k) or home equity play a secondary role. This situation demands a unique approach to financial planning tailored to the entrepreneurial journey.

Ever wonder why a wealth manager wouldn't talk to you about your business, but instead focuses on arbitrary investment performance over arbitrary periods? I think it's because *they're* not playing the same game as you. I call that "playing small ball." This kind of thinking is unfortunate because your business is the single most valuable asset on your personal balance sheet and the single biggest risk asset in your portfolio. Financial advisors are great at asking you to add more money to your accounts. What if they focused on enhancing the value of your single largest financial transaction by getting you personally prepared, and then on managing your newfound wealth? That's playing big ball.

Imagine this: Once your business is sold, it's much like a horse that has bolted from the barn—trying to get things back in order becomes a daunting task, if not an impossible one. The sale of your business is more than just a financial transaction; it's a significant life event that impacts every aspect of your world. If your personal financial, tax, and estate plans aren't discussed well in advance, you could find yourself facing challenges and limited choices that could have been avoided. You may also leave Uncle Sam a large tip in the process.

The key is to act now, before the sale, not after. By getting your personal affairs in order early, you're not just preventing future headaches; you're striving to ensure that your life post-sale is as rewarding and regret-free as possible.

Think of me not just as a wealth manager, but as your partner in this journey. As a business owner myself, I stand with you, shoulder to shoulder. I understand the path you're on because I've walked it too. Together, we'll navigate this journey, ensuring that when you're ready to make that exit, you do so with confidence and a clear vision for the future.

BUILDING DREAMS FROM THE BEGINNING

My entrepreneurial spirit was kindled early, deeply influenced by my parents. As a child, I watched my father wrestle with job after job until he eventually built his own business. Being there for the peaks and valleys, I understood the stark realities of money. My parents eventually decided to exit the rat race and build their business together. These experiences, along with long car rides and "dream building" (going to see houses and cars we couldn't afford) while listening to sales and motivational tapes with my folks, shaped my understanding of financial freedom. I learned it to be something you actively build that isn't dependent on someone else.

High school further fueled my entrepreneurial drive, with books like Napoleon Hill's *Think & Grow Rich* inspiring dreams of starting my own karate studio. However, God had other plans. I found myself studying music education in college, which led to a fulfilling role as a middle school choral conductor. That role, though seemingly distant from my entrepreneurial aspirations, was a pivotal part of my journey. It taught me humility and honed my ability to prioritize—skills that have been invaluable in understanding what money can and cannot do and shaping my approach to wealth management.

These early experiences, from my family's entrepreneurial spirit to my initial career in music, were not detours but foundational steps. They fostered an entrepreneurial mindset within me and a deep understanding of the real value of money—insights that now drive my passion for helping others through my work.

A PARTNER IN PRIORITIZATION

Transitioning from a choral conductor to a wealth manager might seem like a leap, but the core skill of prioritization is a common thread that has woven these two careers together.

In the world of choral music, particularly with the exuberant energy of eighty middle school singers, every rehearsal is a complex puzzle. (If you have a middle-schooler, you get this.) With a concert just around the corner, the pressure intensifies, demanding a sharp focus on what will make the most significant impact. It's about quickly discerning which sections need more practice, which harmonies require fine-tuning, and where the singers need encouragement.

This skill translates seamlessly into wealth management. Just like in a choir where each voice plays a crucial role, each financial decision and investment choice holds its weight in a client's financial picture. The ability to prioritize becomes vital. In the financial realm, this skill is essential for identifying the most pressing needs of a client, understanding the urgency of various financial goals, and recognizing the importance of balancing risk with reward.

In both roles, the essence of prioritization is not just about choosing what to do but also recognizing *what to set aside* for the moment. It's about creating harmony, whether in a piece of music or a client's financial life. The knack for making these judgment calls, honed in the rehearsal room, now plays out for the families I serve. Every family, like every choir, has a unique composition and needs a conductor who can bring out their best. My experience as a conductor has been instrumental in shaping this ability, by allowing me to orchestrate my clients' financial success with the same precision and passion I once held while directing a choir.

FROM CONDUCTOR TO ENTREPRENEUR AND WEALTH MANAGER

My journey from a middle school choral conductor to a wealth manager for entrepreneurs began with a realization: Success in my teaching career wouldn't impact my salary. This led me to embrace my entrepreneurial spirit. I started a community music school, which grew into two locations, and eventually sold. After leaving public education and selling my business without professional guidance, I ventured into podcasting and gained recognition in the conductor community.

A conversation with a friend about marketing his wealth management firm through podcasting piqued my interest in finance. My experience at a large national firm revealed a gap in services for business owners, who are often rich on paper but underserved in practical financial advice—an industry primarily focused on W-2 retirees with a 401(k). Realizing I could serve all clients better as an independent wealth manager, I decided to forge my path.

THE ROAD AHEAD WITH GOLDFIN GROUP

This led to the creation of Goldfin Group, which is dedicated to serving entrepreneurs in various stages: pre-exit, post-exit, and those building lifestyle businesses. Our focus at Goldfin Group is on the unique needs of these entrepreneurs, especially those approaching a business exit.

Permission to Exit is designed for you, the pre-exit entrepreneur. This book aims to guide you through the intricacies of preparing for a successful business exit. Each chapter addresses key areas of your financial plan, complete with actionable steps. As you read, I invite you to consider me to be your resource and guide in navigating this critical phase of your entrepreneurial journey.

CHAPTER ONE

LAYING THE FOUNDATIONS OF SUCCESS

If you don't have the time to do it right, when will you have the time to do it over?

~John Wooden

I mentioned in the introduction that I worked for a large national firm before starting Goldfin Group. When I worked there, I was approached by a man named Mark (not his real name) who wanted to work with me. His wife told me he was getting unsolicited offers to buy his company, and they were north of $50 million.

Odd as it sounds, I told him, "I actually need you to *not* work with me right now." I couldn't tell him I was going independent because of the restrictive covenants of my contract. All I could tell him was that I wanted to work with him, but I couldn't right then.

Mark was in his mid-thirties, and by the time I was ready to begin working with him, he was getting letters of intent from strategic buyers (competitors) and financial buyers (private equity firms) who were interested in acquiring his business.

I went independent shortly thereafter, and we were able to start working together. He had engaged with a mergers and acquisitions (M&A) firm whose advisor fee was quite a bit higher than the market average. I regret not being able to help him vet the firm.

An important detail to note at this point in the story is that the first offer is usually the *highest* offer. When the acquiring firm starts "kicking the tires" and examining the business in more detail, there's a lot to talk about as they pick through your files, look at your organizational systems, figure out what happened in this or that year. Value adjustments are likely to occur as a result of due diligence.

Recognizing the limitations of my role in assisting Mark, I insisted we meet with an estate attorney together to ensure the most important aspects of his estate planning were addressed. As of the writing of this book, we are still in the process of finalizing his estate plan. Mark is a busy man. Upon reflecting, I am reminded of the value I can bring from the onset of the exit planning processes. Had I been involved from the beginning, my expertise could have potentially saved Mark a substantial amount in current and future taxes and spared him from considerable stress.

WHAT MIGHT HAVE BEEN

Mark's exit was impressive—a testament to his hard work and dedication. It was undoubtedly a success, and he has every reason to be proud. Yet, a crucial element was missing in the lead-up to the sale: the right team and timing. Being deeply involved in the sale process often leaves little room to focus on other critical aspects.

The remarkable thing about Mark's story is the timing of his professional and personal milestones. He became the CEO of a significantly expanded team, courtesy of a private equity fund, at the very moment his wife was giving birth to twins. His life was busier than ever, managing both an expanding company and a growing family.

With such a hectic schedule, finding time for additional planning was nearly impossible. Had Mark taken a moment earlier to thoroughly plan the sale of his business, he might have not only saved a significant amount in taxes but also reduced his anxiety and created more space for himself post-sale.

I often think about how beneficial it would have been for Mark to have access to the insights in this book a year or two before he even considered selling. It would have equipped him with the knowledge and foresight to make more informed decisions.

In hindsight, I wish I could have been there earlier to help Mark position himself for an even greater win. Teaching the importance of early and thorough preparation is one of the key principles I advocate, and it's designed to help entrepreneurs like Mark achieve the best possible outcomes in their business exits.

WHAT IS SWING THEORY?

One evening in Franklin, Tennessee, I was dining with Doug, a fellow business owner and friend. As we discussed my role in aiding entrepreneurs both pre-and-post-liquidity, Doug, who was contemplating selling his business, posed a thought-provoking question: "How does one know when it's the right time to sell?"

In that moment, I spontaneously devised what I now call "Swing Theory"—a proud moment of improvisation on my part. This theory offers a solid framework for selling your business without regrets.

Remember how exhilarating it was to play on the swings as a child? The thrill lay in timing your jump to maximize airtime and ensure a smooth landing. The tricky part was in perfecting the timing at the very top of the swing's arc, so the best strategy was often to jump while on the way up.

In my opinion, this analogy applies to business sales. Ideally, every owner wants to exit during an upward trajectory. However, pinpointing the peak—the "top" of the swing—is difficult. It's much like trying to time the market by holding cash and waiting for the right time to buy (which is nearly impossible to do).

On top of that, it's morally responsible to pass the baton while the business is thriving, in an attempt to ensure a fair and optimistic transition.

From a negotiating standpoint, it's also advantageous to engage in sale discussions during a growth phase. Attempting to sell during a downturn undermines your bargaining position, as potential buyers may be hesitant to invest in a business that appears to be declining in value. Would you board a sinking ship?

Therefore, ethically and financially, the smart move is to sell while your business is on the upswing. This approach not only allows you to sell with assurance, but also propels you energetically into your next venture, bolstered by the success of a *well-timed* (or not timed at all) exit.

Though it may seem straightforward, the truth is that many entrepreneurs overlook the immense value of thoughtful exit planning. Let's delve into some reasons why this is so crucial.

WHY DO ENTREPRENEURS PUT OFF EXIT PLANNING?

Let's explore some of the most common reasons entrepreneurs don't give their attention to *personally* planning their exit. My guess is that you'll relate to at least a few of these.

Emotional Attachment: Many entrepreneurs see their businesses as their life's work and struggle with the idea of letting go. This emotional attachment can make the thought of exit planning feel like giving up a part of themselves.

Identity Concerns: Many business owners' personal identity is closely tied to their business. The thought of not being the owner, CEO, or the face of the company can lead to existential worries about who they are without their company.

Lack of Time: Entrepreneurs are often consumed by the day-to-day operations of their business. Finding time to plan for an exit can seem like a lower priority, especially if they are heavily involved in the ongoing activities of the company.

Overconfidence in Business Viability: Some business owners may believe that their business will always be successful under their helm, leading them to postpone planning for a future that doesn't involve them.

Uncertainty About the Future: Uncertainty about what they would do post-exit can be daunting. The fear of the unknown and what lies beyond the business can be a significant deterrent.

Perception of Early Planning: Some entrepreneurs might think it's too early to start planning their exit, especially if they don't foresee leaving or selling the business in the immediate future.

Complexity and Overwhelm: The process of exit planning can seem overwhelming and complex. This can lead to procrastination, especially if they're unsure of where to start.

Fear of Financial Security: Concerns about ensuring financial stability post-exit can be a significant worry, particularly if the business is the primary source of income. In essence, it's shutting off the familiar ATM to their life.

Losing Control over Effort: There's a certain sense of freedom from being the one in control of the effort that makes the money come quicker or slower. Having some control over effort makes it harder to quit or say enough is enough.

Successor Uncertainty: Worries about the business's future under different leadership (not them) can stall the planning process.

Underestimating the Importance: Some entrepreneurs may not fully understand the benefits of exit planning, viewing it as unnecessary until the need arises.

Market Timing Concerns: Waiting for the right time in terms of market conditions or business valuation can lead to delays.

Reluctance to Seek Advice: A hesitancy to consult with deal people like investment bankers, business brokers, lawyers, or other professionals for guidance can also be a barrier.

That's quite a list! It's helpful to understand the myriad of reasons why we avoid things that are important to us. Yet it's even more important to take action and begin.

CONSIDER PLANNING NOW

Have you ever had a family vacation on the calendar for months, but it seemed to sneak up on you at the last minute? You'd gotten so busy living life that this important family event seemed to materialize out of nowhere. If you're like me, you stayed up late to pack the night before and got about four hours of sleep, even though the trip had been on the calendar for months.

The same can happen with your business exit. You know it's out there on the horizon somewhere, and with each passing year you become more aware that you need to put some thoughtful plans in motion. However, you've been so busy running the business that you haven't taken adequate time to plan, or even think it through.

We'll talk about more specific details in subsequent chapters. But for now, I'd like you to consider several benefits of starting your planning now.

Control Over the Exit Process: Early planning puts you in the driver's seat. You can dictate the terms and timeline of the exit rather than being reactive to market conditions or unforeseen events.

Maximizing Business Value: By planning ahead, you can implement strategies to improve your business's financial health and operational efficiency, ultimately enhancing its value when it's time to sell. Keep in mind that your business is likely the most significant chunk of your net worth.

Strategic Timing: Starting early allows you to time your exit to coincide with optimal market conditions, the performance of your business (see Swing Theory), or personal life events, striving toward a more favorable outcome.

Reduced Stress and Better Decision-Making: With a plan in place, you can avoid the rushed decisions and stress that often come with last-minute exit planning. You'll have the luxury of time to consider all options and make informed decisions. Remember, financial buyers are among some of the most highly educated and sophisticated entrepreneurs on the planet. You need to bring your A-game.

Preparing for Life After Business: Early planning allows you to explore and develop personal interests and passions outside the business. This can make the transition out of your business role smoother and more fulfilling.

Handling Unforeseen Circumstances: Life is unpredictable. Early exit planning helps you and your business to be better prepared for unexpected events, such as health issues or economic downturns.

Opportunity for Tax Optimization: Planning ahead provides more opportunities for tax planning strategies that can significantly reduce tax liabilities associated with the sale or transfer of the business.

Attracting Quality Offers: A well-planned exit strategy can make your business more attractive to potential buyers or investors because you, the owner, are more confident. It also demonstrates a well-run business with a clear future path, which can lead to better offers.

Peace of Mind: Perhaps one of the most significant benefits is the peace of mind that comes with knowing you have a plan in place for one of the most critical transitions in your life.

Regret Avoidance: Knowing you did a great job planning will help you avoid seller's remorse—more or less the subtitle of this book.

Most importantly, *Financial Security and Clarity:* Early planning helps clarify the financial implications of the exit. It allows you the opportunity to develop a well-defined financial plan for the post-exit phase, contributing to your financial stability and the achievement of personal objectives.

As you can see, there are huge benefits to planning ahead. But it doesn't need to be an overly complicated process. It just requires a bit of intentional thinking and forethought.

In the next chapter, we'll dig into several key areas that will greatly impact how you think about your exit in terms of your family, core values, and purpose.

ACTION ITEMS

1. List all the reasons *you* don't want to start planning right now. What's standing in your way?
2. List the potential personal consequences (for you) of not planning your business exit on your terms.
3. List the consequences to others (your family, employees, vendors, your current customers, etc.) if you don't exit well.

CHAPTER TWO

ALIGNING FAMILY, VALUES, AND MISSION

But the fruit of the Spirit is love, joy, peace, patience, kindness, goodness, faithfulness, gentleness, self-control; against such things, there is no law.

Galatians 5:22-23, NASB

Back when I lived in New York City, and before I was in the financial industry, I met John at a networking event. He was recently divorced and lived nearby. We struck up a conversation, and he mentioned that a few years back, he'd sold his consulting company for a substantial sum.

At first, it seemed like he was living the dream. But as the conversation continued, it became apparent there was more to his story.

John admitted that after selling his company, he quickly realized he had lost the sense of purpose that had driven him for years. His identity had been so intertwined with his business that without it, he felt lost and directionless.

As a result, he began to struggle with depression, which he now realized took a toll on his relationships.

He recounted how he tried to fill the void with extravagant purchases, like buying an exotic car and a vacation home in Cabo. He also went on a spree of lavish trips, assuming that the thrill of new experiences would bring him happiness.

It didn't.

Instead, John found that his material possessions and indulgences only led to fleeting moments of excitement. These would always be followed by a deepening sense of emptiness once the dopamine wore off.

His lack of purpose also began to affect his marriage. With so much time on his hands, he and his wife found themselves arguing more often as they just seemed to get in each other's way. John admitted that he stirred up trouble because it "probably gave him something to fix."

John's relationship with his children also suffered because they grew resentful of his seemingly endless quest for distractions and entertainment.

John's mental health continued to suffer. He hid the drinking and the other unhealthy coping mechanisms he used to numb the pain of his existential crisis.

He was sabotaging his success.

His family life crumbled, and he found himself feeling more isolated than ever.

He confided that his biggest regret was not having a plan for his life after the sale of his business. He didn't have a passion outside of his business. He told me he wished he had spent time reflecting on what was important to him—his values and mission in life.

Nearly ten years later, I think it would have made a ton of sense to have sought the advice of a professional to help him navigate this significant life transition.

Thankfully, at the time of our conversation, John was pulling his life back together. He started another consulting endeavor and was at the event promoting it. His relationships were also on the mend.

John's story is a cautionary tale that illustrates why it's vital to have a well-defined sense of purpose, core values, and a solid plan in place for your life after selling a business. Without these elements, even the most successful entrepreneurs can find themselves floundering and feeling unfulfilled in spite of their newfound wealth.

THE IMPORTANCE OF CORE VALUES AND PURPOSE

Your *core values* are the principles that govern your behavior and decision-making. Your *purpose* is the overarching reason for your existence. Together, they act as a compass that helps you stay focused on what truly matters and enables you to make choices that align with your beliefs and passions.

When you have a clear understanding of your core values and purpose, you're much more likely to experience a sense of direction and fulfillment in your life.

I've included a list of core values below. While these aren't a definitive list, they capture some of the most important values with which entrepreneurs typically resonate.

You might want to circle the ones that speak to you the most or write them down in a journal for future reference.

Integrity	Compassion	Humility
Family	Generosity	Forgiveness
Faithfulness	Kindness	Gratitude
Love	Patience	Respect
Peace	Empathy	Self-control
Courage	Service	Stewardship
Wisdom	Hope	Accountability
Dependability	Joy	Harmony
Collaboration	Devotion	Balance
Spirituality	Fairness	Purpose
Contentment	Hospitality	Discipline
Gentleness	Modesty	Legacy
Learning	Mindfulness	Benevolence

When you're in the middle of running your business, you feel alive and driven because you've actively engaged in building something. But what happens when you sell your business, and you don't have a clear purpose that transcends the business?

CREATE A PURPOSE STATEMENT

Using your core values as a guide, draft a concise and clear personal purpose statement. Make sure it is specific and actionable so it can serve as a concrete guide for decision-making and goal-setting.

> A simple formula for crafting a personal purpose statement could be:
>
> [Value 1] + [Value 2] + [Value 3] + [Purpose] + [Goal or Aspiration]

For example, using the formula:

Integrity + Service + Empowerment + Inspiring others + Personal growth = "Living a life of integrity and service, using my talents to inspire and empower others, fostering strong relationships and personal growth."

By following this formula, you can create a personal or family purpose statement that captures your core values and purpose, providing a guide for your decisions and goals throughout your life.

Here is my family's purpose statement:

"To lead by example and nurture a loving family, dedicated to faith, generosity, and lifelong learning, while pursuing a fulfilling career that makes a meaningful impact on others."

With a clear purpose, life after selling your business can be fulfilling and values-driven. Entrepreneurs who have a plan for their post-business life often find new avenues for their passion and energy. They experience a sense of renewal and identity beyond their business roles.

After investing years into building your business, transitioning to a life filled with joy and purpose is not only possible, but highly rewarding. This is especially true when you have the financial freedom as a result of a successful business sale.

Ultimately, this transition allows you to enrich the lives of those you love most—the very people for whom you built your business. With thoughtful planning and a forward-looking mindset, you can position yourself so that the end of your business journey may mark the beginning of another exciting chapter in your life.

YOUR MOST IMPORTANT RELATIONSHIPS

As you prepare for your business exit, it's vital to consider the relationships that matter most: your spouse, children, grandchildren, siblings, and aging parents. Remember, after the sale, these are the people you come home to. More than anything, as entrepreneurs, we aspire to instill in our children the traits that fueled our success, while being mindful to avoid fostering a sense of entitlement.

This balancing act is crucial and requires thoughtful planning. Establishing clear family values and what you stand for is essential, especially before wealth changes the dynamics. In my family, for instance, we use a Bible verse as our guiding principle. This helps us stay grounded in our values as our children grow. You might choose a different anchor, but the goal is the same: to define what values will steer your family's course.

This is not just about avoiding the trap of "Keeping up with the Joneses" but about laying a foundation for what truly matters. Think deeply about what you wish to pass on to your children. Many entrepreneurs are careful about not giving their children everything on a silver platter, understanding that hardships and challenges shape character.

Your responsibility often extends beyond your immediate family. For many, especially in middle age, this includes aging parents. The dynamics in every family are different, but it's important to consider your role in their care, particularly if you are seen as the most dependable among your siblings.

In essence, before you dive into the complexities of a business sale, take time to reflect on these relationships. What legacy do you want to leave? Are you expressing gratitude for your blessings today? Do your kids see you serving others? Do they serve others themselves? Are they getting adequate perspective?

These are the types of questions that are useful to ponder today.

THE POWER OF NON-BUSINESS GOALS

While you were busy building the business, you probably had little time for anything outside of work and family. But now that you're considering an exit, take some time to think about your goals and interests outside of your business.

You could probably name a dozen business goals off the top of your head, but I'll bet you would struggle to name a dozen non-business goals. These could be going on a regular date night with your spouse, coaching your kid's baseball or soccer team, or finally putting that engine back in the Trans Am in your garage.

Many entrepreneurs are obsessed with the game of business. But there are other games, too. Play some other games.

Those are the things you'll be glad you did when you're on your deathbed. They are the source of much regret if you don't do them.

You would never hear an entrepreneur at the end of their life say, "I wish I had hit that earnings before interest, taxes, depreciation, and amortization multiple on the sale of my first business." You'd be more likely to hear, "I wish I had spent more time with my father before he passed. There were so many more stories to tell, and I wish I'd known him better."

Or it might be, "I wish I would have been more available for my kids. I feel like I missed their younger years." That's an arrow through the heart, isn't it?

As everyone tells you, time goes by faster and faster as you get older, especially when you have kids. Slow down and take your kids along with you. Involve your spouse. Spend time with your aging parents. Those are the relationships you'll be left with after the excitement of selling your business wears off.

THE BRUTAL TRUTH

Post-sale, managing relationships can become more complex with increased wealth. The proverbial walls of your *castle* may need to be higher, the *moat* deeper, as affluence often brings heightened attention. The distinction between envy and admiration can blur; many might look at your luxury possessions, like a Rolex or a Porsche 911, and imagine themselves in your place.

Moreover, wealth can cloud the authenticity of relationships. It's challenging to discern whether someone is genuinely interested in you or primarily attracted to your financial status. People who are aware of your wealth may become overly flattering, motivated by the prospect of personal gain. This dynamic makes it increasingly important to develop a keen sense of discernment in your interactions, separating genuine interest from opportunistic behavior.

That's why it's critical to take time now, before your exit, to think deeply about the relationships that matter most.

In the next chapter, we'll have the opportunity to get clear on your financial picture, so you have a sense of what you need out of the sale of your business to maintain your lifestyle or even give it an upgrade.

ACTION ITEMS

1. On a scale of 1-5, take a relationship inventory. Ask your immediate family how you're doing in your role at home by using the following questions.

   - Availability: "How available do you feel I am for you when you need me? This includes being there for important events, being emotionally present during conversations, and being accessible when you want to talk or spend time together."

   - Supportiveness: "How would you rate my supportiveness in your endeavors and challenges? Consider how I respond to your needs, whether I offer help and encouragement, and if I'm there to listen and assist when facing difficulties."

   - Quality Time: "Rate the quality of the time we spend together. Think about our activities, conversations, and how engaged and involved I am during our time together."

   - Understanding and Empathy: "How well do you think I understand your feelings and perspectives? Consider my ability to empathize with you, to genuinely comprehend your experiences, and to react sensitively to your emotions."

- Fun and Enjoyment: "Rate how enjoyable and fun our interactions are. Think about whether I contribute positively to our family environment, if we share laughs and joy, and if you look forward to our time together."

After receiving their ratings, you can follow up with an open-ended question like, "What can I do more of to improve in these areas?" (Note: "more of" are the operative words. Keep it positive.)

You can download a relationship inventory in this book's bonuses at Goldfin.Group/ExitBook.

2. Talk to your family about your earliest money memory. Describe how it shapes the way you look at money's role in your life. You might be surprised at what comes to mind when you start digging into your memories.

3. Talk to your spouse about whether each of you feels rich. How would each of you define rich? If you're not, what would it take for you to feel that way? (Note: Is it a money answer? Is it an answer about wealth relative to others? Is it a time answer, or something else?)

4. Take an inventory of all the people who rely on you for money. Who do you have a moral obligation to provide for if they can't provide for themselves?

CHAPTER THREE

CRAFTING YOUR FINANCIAL BLUEPRINT

The trouble with not having a goal is that you can spend your life running up and down the field and never score.

~Bill Copeland

Let me introduce you to Stanley (not his real name), a driven entrepreneur who built his success as a basement remodeling contractor. He started his business in his late teens, targeting a specific demand in home renovation. His keen sense of market trends led him to expand his operations, eventually growing his business to a remarkable scale. When we began our collaboration, his business's EBITDA, or in simpler terms, the profit before certain expenses, was around $3 million.

Stanley's success was rooted in his commitment to quality workmanship, efficient project management, and strategic expansion. Known for transforming basements into exceptional [and dry] living spaces, his business became a go-to in the industry.

In working with Stanley, and with all our clients, we follow Goldfin's three-step process, designed to provide clarity and precision in our approach. First, it all begins with a simple conversation—an introductory call with us. This initial chat is crucial; it's where we begin to understand your current situation and aspirations. Second, if there's mutual interest in proceeding, we delve deeper in a discovery meeting. This second step involves a more comprehensive discussion where you can share in detail about your personal circumstances, business, and goals.

The third step is where your plan begins to take form. In our third conversation, we present you with a "number"—a specific financial target that aligns with your post-exit objectives and what you may need from your business sale. We also outline a path to help you reach this target, customized to your unique situation. This structured yet personalized approach is designed to assist you so that, by the time you're ready to make significant decisions about your business exit, you have a clear, actionable plan to guide you.

At various points throughout the process, we'll make introductions to potential team members and partners that will help you get crucial activities done well ahead of the sale. We'll even attend those meetings with you to make sure nothing slips through the cracks.

Not long after joining forces with us, Stanley decided it was time to leverage his hard work through a sale. He sought a structured exit strategy to maximize his business's value and ensure its ongoing success.

I led Stanley's financial team, bringing together a diverse group of professionals, including an investment banker, an M&A attorney, a tax advisor, and a trust and estate attorney. Our focus was on aligning the sale with Stanley's personal and financial goals, following Goldfin's three-step process. We closely examined his financial situation and future aspirations, determining his *number*—the price tag he needed from the sale after all taxes and fees—to walk away without regret.

With a comprehensive valuation of his business, the team pinpointed areas to boost its value before the sale. This led to a confident negotiation with a private equity buyer, even though we anticipated that the initial high offers might be adjusted post-due diligence.

After the sale, the transition to the new owners was smooth, ensuring continuity for both clients and employees. It wasn't long before my team was wiring $15 million into he and his wife's trust account at my office.

By implementing thoughtful investment and wealth preservation strategies, Stanley aimed to create a secure financial future. This approach was not just about seeking a successful exit but also about gaining the flexibility to pursue new opportunities and interests.

Today, Stanley is leveraging his entrepreneurial skills in a new venture focusing on air purification technology, while balancing his professional ambitions with quality time for his family. He also mentors aspiring entrepreneurs, sharing his rich experience in building and selling a business.

Reflecting on his successful exit, Stanley feels fulfilled. His story is a testament to the power of strategic planning and sanctioning a dedicated financial team in navigating the complexities of selling a thriving business. Stanley's journey underscores the essence of what I like to call *The Goldfin Moment:* achieving a successful, regret-free exit that sets the stage for future endeavors and a balanced life. His experience underscores the value of early and thorough planning. Such planning aims to support not only potential financial stability but also personal fulfillment after exiting the business.

I want the same for you. But as I've emphasized throughout this book, it doesn't happen by accident. It involves a great deal of planning and forethought. As the title of this book suggests, you must *prepare* to exit before you get *permission* to exit.

In order to do that, you need to be clear on four critical numbers that comprise your overall financial picture. Let's explore each of these and why they're so important.

1. YOUR BUSINESS VALUE

In the simplest terms, your business value is what your business is worth.

As an entrepreneur growing a business, it's easy to get emotionally wrapped up in the thing you created. Therefore, this is a good time to be as objective as you can. Every business can be quantified with a specific range of monetary value.

Unfortunately, many people who are looking to exit their business use the wrong benchmarks to determine their business's value. I often see clients fixate on a number because a friend of theirs sold for a similar number. We call that *anchoring bias*. There are a handful of other biases that come into play when dealing with someone's closely held business.

This is why you need to speak with a professional to help you evaluate it. You will want a preliminary valuation, just like a real estate broker will provide a comparative market analysis for you before they attempt to list your home for sale. That way, you know what number to attach to a listing. It's part of my process to make introductions to the professionals who provide this service.

Your business value should be recent and based on current market conditions informed by a professional.

2. YOUR NET WORTH

Your net worth is everything you *own* minus everything you *owe*. This is listed on your personal balance sheet, comprising assets (own) and liabilities (owe).

Your assets include everything you own that has value: your primary home, vacation home, bank account balances, 401(k)s, IRAs, Roth IRAs, brokerage accounts, etc. It also includes that piece of land you're not sure you'll ever do anything with but purchased because it seemed like a good deal.

Of course, your asset column also includes the value of your business. Your tax advisor might have given you a value for tax, estate, financial reporting, or legal purposes. What a tax advisor provides is different from an investment banker's valuation. They're serving two different audiences and using two different methodologies.

What about the things you owe money on? That includes your mortgage, car payments, student loans, any other debts, and other loans you might have personally guaranteed for others or for yourself, such as an SBA (Small Business Administration) loan. Your most recent credit report should show all the items you've personally guaranteed that have outstanding balances.

Since you're reading this book about making a business exit, I assume that you own more than you owe. In other words, you have a positive net worth.

3. YOUR PERSONAL EXPENSES

In addition to your business value and your net worth, it's important to have a clear picture of your personal expenses.

What does your personal cash flow situation look like? Your standard of living is based on how much money flows into your personal account versus how much leaves it. What do you take out of the business each year, money-wise, to meet your family's spending needs and wants?

You likely pay yourself a salary in your role as the business owner. Then, you probably take a draw from the business to cover anything over and above your salary. It's vital to see how much you actually take out of the business each year in order to fund your life.

We're talking about your standard of living. What does it cost today to cover all your expenses? Is this standard of living one you want to continue? Do you feel like you need to downgrade or upgrade post-sale?

As you're determining the amount you need to cover personal expenses, make sure to include everything. There are regular monthly items such as a mortgage, electric bill, college tuition, groceries, perhaps a car payment, etc.

It's easy to miss other more discretionary expenses like vacations, hobbies, and perhaps your family's shopping habits. If you don't include those, you're not really quantifying your true standard of living.

I often put it this way for my clients. Let's say that we shut off the ATM altogether, and I needed to write you a check every month for everything you wanted to do to sustain your lifestyle. How much does that monthly check need to be to support you and your family?

If you're going to err, do it on the conservative side of this number. It needs to be a little bigger than your first inclination, which may be to go simple and assume you don't need a whole lot. But once you have a firm idea of this number, it helps you determine the next item, which is the number we've been building toward.

4. YOUR EXIT NUMBER

After you sell the business and pay the taxes and fees, what's left? You'll need an answer to number three to do this one right. We want to understand what it will take to sustain your lifestyle beyond the sale.

You've grown accustomed to a particular lifestyle, so let's make sure you can, at the very least, continue it. It's also helpful to understand and predict what might change on the other side of that exit.

Let me share a simple formula for figuring out your exit number, with the caveat that it's more complex than this. The right wealth manager can be a great help in walking you through the nuances of determining this number at a more granular level. That said, my goal is to help you do some "back of the napkin" math today.

A useful guideline for estimating your financial needs post-business sale is a modified version of "The 4% Rule." This rule is traditionally used for retirement planning, where you can safely withdraw 4% of your retirement savings each year, for a 30-year retirement, out of a diversified portfolio of 60% stocks/40% bonds. Everyone has their interpretation of the 4% Rule, the mix of stocks to bonds, and how or when they take withdrawals. For this book, it's a reasonable place to start. To use this rule for calculating your exit number, consider your desired annual pre-tax income that you'll need to maintain your current lifestyle, assuming you never make another dollar in your life.

For instance, if you aim for an annual income of $500,000 to sustain your lifestyle, you will multiply this amount by twenty-five. This calculation is based on the inverse of The 4% Rule, indicating how much total capital you need to safely withdraw 4% annually. In this case, you would need a net exit amount of $12,500,000 from the sale of your business.

This figure, however, is just a starting point. It assumes that your annual expenses will increase by 3% each year, to account for inflation, and that the proceeds are invested in a moderate growth portfolio of investments.

Additionally, you should consider any significant one-time expenses you plan to cover with the proceeds. For example, if you want to pay off a $1,000,000 mortgage or purchase a $750,000 airplane, these amounts should be added to the initial $12,500,000. Remember, ongoing costs like maintenance, insurance, and fuel for the airplane should be included in your annual $500,000 budget. If they're not, you will need to increase your $500,000 budget accordingly and multiply by twenty-five again, then add your one-time purchases or expenses back.

Finally, it's crucial to remember that the $12,500,000 should be the amount you receive after all taxes, fees, and other costs associated with the sale. The actual sale price of your business will likely need to be significantly higher (let's say 33%) to net this amount.

The math would look like $12,500,000 x 1.33 = $16,625,000.

By considering these factors, you can develop a more accurate and comprehensive financial plan for your life post-business sale.

We've covered a lot of ground in this chapter! The good news, though, is that once you have clarity about these four figures—your business value, your net worth, your personal expenses, and your exit number—you will be better equipped to make decisions about your exit.

Before we start thinking about exit specifics, let's turn our attention to taking a long-term perspective on investing, wealth, and success. This will set the stage for the rest of the book.

ACTION ITEMS

1. Do a "back of the napkin" personal balance sheet. Draw a line down the center of a sheet of paper. Put assets on one side, liabilities on the other. Subtract what you owe (liabilities) from what you own (assets). That's your net worth. Remember that your business interest is in the ownership (asset) column. What percent of your family's net worth is the business? (Note: It will take more than the back of a napkin if you want to do this perfectly, so aim for "good enough" if you're not an Excel guru.)

2. Figure out what you actually spend each month. The easiest way to do this is to look at what monthly bank drafts come out of your account each month and list them. Add to that your average monthly credit card bill.

   A common pitfall is only looking at *necessary* or non-discretionary expenses and not factoring in the lifestyle expenses you've grown accustomed to, like vacations or nice dinners. The main data you're gathering here is what your life costs you to live every month, on average.

3. What about the above would change if you got what you wanted for your business? The answers to these questions will be helpful as we figure out your exit number.

    - List the one-time purchases and put a price tag on each.
    - List the ongoing payments and what they would be used for.
    - List what you would do differently if you had the money available.

4. Figure out your number using the methodology above, then email it to me here: Ryan@Goldfin.Group. I'm curious to know the number from people who are reading this book.

CHAPTER FOUR

INVESTING WITH A LONG-TERM OUTLOOK

The stock market is a device for transferring money from the impatient to the patient.
~Warren Buffett

Although this book is focused on the short-to-medium-term goal of your business exit, I also want you to think about your financial picture beyond the sale—the stage where we spend most of our time partnering with clients.

When you exit and receive a huge check (or wire, which sounds less exciting, to be honest), it can feel overwhelming. You've been waiting for this moment since you started building your business. Now that you've sold, it can almost feel like you are set for life.

However, remember, the skills and perhaps a touch of divine providence that helped you build wealth aren't the same tools you'll need to maintain it. Long-term wealth building requires a shift in approach, focusing on investor *behavior* over time.

Building passive wealth is based on quantity and time: the amount of money you invest, plus the compounding returns over time. You have been a successful entrepreneur, in part, because you are *impatient*. You take action and get results. You took risks others wouldn't dare, and probably ignored the advice of naysayers and doubters many times.

Take an honest look at your tendencies. When it comes to the long-term outlook of other peoples' companies (the publicly traded ones) that happen to be marked to market every millisecond of every trading day, do you have a tendency to judge or even play Monday morning quarterback with your opinions? Are you prone to investing fads? Did those non-fungible tokens (NFTs) put your kids through college, or are they about as valuable as my Beanie Baby collection from 1996? Where do you get your financial or economic news? What is the general tone or outlook of those sources? How do you react to such information?

This is where entrepreneurs can blow themselves up. Investing for the long haul is a different game. It's less about immediate action and more about patience and time. Entrepreneurs often thrive on being in control, yet the nature of investing in a diversified portfolio of low-cost exchange-traded funds requires a shift in perspective. It's about embracing patience over direct control.

Think about your company today. Would you want your company marked to market every minute you're open, five days a week, with news analysts painting a picture of your company to the public based on whatever fits the advertising narrative of the day? How many press conferences would you need to have if MSNBC or Fox Business camped out in your HR director's office looking for a scoop?

See what I'm saying?

With that perspective in mind, let's explore an example that highlights the importance of patience and a steady approach to building lasting wealth.

BEFORE I SAY THE WORD *MARKET* AGAIN:

The term *market*, as commonly used in financial discussions, is somewhat of a misnomer, particularly when it's referenced in the context of investment strategies like those of John and Sarah (our next example). Often, when people talk about "the market," they are referring to a specific segment of the global financial system, predominantly the market for large U.S. companies listed on major stock exchanges. This market is not just any marketplace, but a highly dynamic and influential one, driven by some of the world's most innovative and successful entrepreneurs.

It's important to clarify that this market is not a broad or generic concept. Instead, it represents a specific and significant part of the global economic ecosystem. These companies are at the forefront of global business and innovation, and their performance significantly impacts investors' strategies and the overall perception of market health and trends.

In summary, the term market in this context is more accurately understood as a reference to the vibrant and influential market of major U.S. companies, a sector that plays a crucial role in investment decisions and economic discussions worldwide.

UNDERSTANDING MARKET TIMING AND ITS RISKS

When investors consider entering or exiting the market, one of the most significant challenges they face is the unpredictability of market fluctuations. This unpredictability is particularly evident when comparing the investment approaches of two totally made-up investors, John and Sarah, who each have their own strategies during market ups and downs. It's important to note that both John and Sarah have long-term time horizons (think: decades).

Sarah, reacting to market volatility, decides to sell her investments during a downturn and waits on the sidelines with cash, hoping to re-enter the market when it seems more stable. John, on the other hand, maintains his investment regardless of short-term market movements, adhering to a long-term investment strategy.

Fast forward several years and the outcomes of their decisions become apparent. Sarah, who attempted to time the market, missed out on crucial periods of market recovery. Her decision to exit and later re-enter the market meant she was not invested during some of the market's best performing days. In contrast, John's approach of staying invested allowed him to experience both the declines and the recoveries.

The challenge with Sarah's approach lies in the fact that the market's best performing days often occur unexpectedly and can be concentrated within very short time frames. Missing these key days can significantly impact the overall return of an investment portfolio. Historical data[1] shows that these peak recovery days often happen close to the market's worst days, making the timing of exits and entries particularly challenging.

---

1 Source: FactSet. Daily data from January 3, 1928 through December 30, 2022. Past performance is no guarantee of future results. It is not possible to invest in an index.

The risk of missing the market's best days serves as a critical reminder of the difficulties associated with market timing. It emphasizes the importance of a consistent, long-term investment perspective. Staying invested through market cycles allows investors to be present for these high-return days, versus attempting to avoid downturns by moving in and out of the market which can lead to missed opportunities, potentially hindering the long-term growth of an investment portfolio.

At the end of the day, the tale of John and Sarah, which highlights the risks of missing the market's best days, underscores the value of a steady, long-term approach to investing. It highlights the importance of aligning investment strategies with long-term goals and risk tolerance, rather than trying to predict short-term market movements.

THE BEAUTY OF LONG-TERM INVESTING

Here's another perspective to keep in mind, especially when you think about investing in publicly held U.S. equities. The CEO and board of directors have a fiduciary obligation to their shareholders to continue being good stewards of that business. Plus, they must either return profits to you (dividends), use those profits to grow the company's value, or a combination of both.

They are riding alongside you on the company's value journey. If the business value goes up, you get richer, and so do they. It's a win-win for all parties. It pays to be an optimist.

That's hard to keep in mind when things aren't going well for a company. However, when bad things happen, companies get better. Owners and leaders want to work on problems until they are fixed.

Take airplanes, for example. Every time there's a crash, airplanes get safer because we learn something from the black box. On a side note, why haven't we learned to make planes out of the black box material? (Kidding.)

When it comes to value declines, I often remind my clients, "If you only ever inhaled, you would explode. You have to exhale every once in a while." It's true of nature, and it's true of public markets.

ALLOWING FOR SOME LEEWAY

In wealth management, we often look to historical market trends to inform our strategies. Historical data shows that the stock market experiences significant fluctuations over time. For instance, according to data from Fidelity Investments, in their piece *Market Volatility is Normal: Staying the Course is Critical*, historically, from 1980 through the end of 2022, the S&P 500® Index had a positive return in thirty-five of the last forty-three years—more than 81% of the time. The index returned an average of 13% per year. While past performance is not indicative of future results, and it's not possible to invest directly into an index itself, understanding these patterns can be useful for setting realistic expectations.

Additionally, when examining the S&P 500's historical performance from 1980 to 2022, it's noted that the average intra-year decline (measured from a peak to a trough within a single year) is around 14%. This means that if you have a portfolio entirely composed of equities, seeing it fluctuate by about 14% within a year aligns with historical trends.

Moreover, it's not uncommon to observe at least one 10% correction in any given year.

It's important to understand these historical trends as they underscore the normalcy of market volatility. This knowledge can be pivotal in maintaining a long-term perspective and avoiding reactive decisions based on short-term market movements.

Think of your investment journey like planning a long road trip from Nashville to Los Angeles. In this travel analogy, you wouldn't measure the trip in inches but in miles because it's a significant distance. Similarly, when considering your financial journey, it's more practical to view it in broader terms rather than obsessing over every small fluctuation.

Just as you wouldn't focus on every interstate mile marker during your trip—unless you want to make the journey tedious—the same principle applies to monitoring the value of your investments. As an entrepreneur, you're familiar with the ups and downs in the value of your company. These fluctuations are a normal part of the business cycle. Likewise, the stock market, comprised of numerous companies led by some of the world's best entrepreneurs, also experiences its peaks and valleys. This is a natural aspect of economic cycles.

It's important to extend the same understanding and patience to these market fluctuations as you would to your own business. The prices of equities, and consequently the value of your portfolio, are influenced by a variety of factors: market conditions, global events, and even our collective human responses to these factors. Recognizing this, it's essential to give these companies, and by extension, your investments, the leeway to navigate through these variables, just as you navigate your business through its challenges. This perspective helps in maintaining a long-term view of your investments, avoiding the stress of reacting to short-term market movements.

In the previous few chapters, we've spent a lot of time talking about the value of your most important possessions—namely, your family and your business. In the following chapter, you'll learn some tools to protect what is most precious to you.

ACTION ITEMS

1. Do a news inventory. Where do you get your financial news? Who are their sponsors? How do you think what you are reading, watching, and listening to is influenced by the agenda of the sponsors? When you read a negative headline, how do you typically react?

2. Do an influence inventory. Who do you talk to about financial and economic news or ideas? What is *their* financial situation? Do you want to be like them? What economic/business problems or opportunities do you have in common?

3. Unsubscribe from news outlets that have a tendency to affect your day. This might mean setting up your environment for success by blocking certain news websites and turning off settings on your phone or computer that default to news outlets. Maybe it means finding a new favorite podcast or radio station, subscribing to an audiobook platform, and replacing what you listen to with uplifting or interesting books, or throwing your TV out the window.

CHAPTER FIVE

SAFEGUARDING YOUR JOURNEY: PROTECTION AND RISK MANAGEMENT

We are very good at predicting the future, except for the surprises—which tend to be all that matter.

~Morgan Housel

The world-renowned musician Prince was famous for decades because of his incredible skills as a musician, songwriter, and performer. But in the aftermath of his shocking death in 2016, he became famous for a whole new reason: He died without an estate plan.

As a result, his sister and half-siblings went to court to determine the rightful heirs. Some of them even went through court-ordered genetic testing to ensure they were actually related to Prince.

With an estate worth hundreds of millions of dollars—not to mention Prince's renowned vault of unpublished music that will take decades to release—it's no surprise that the lack of proper legal documents caused enormous chaos in his family.

Sadly, this isn't unusual. Public figures like Abraham Lincoln, Sonny Bono, Kurt Cobain, Pablo Picasso, and Howard Hughes are just a few names on the notorious list of people who died without an estate plan.

I understand how crucial it is to prevent chaos for your family and those relying on you—like your business partners, employees, and others close to you. Part of preparing for your business exit is striving to improve everyone's security, particularly in unexpected situations. If you're currently without key protections, you're risking not just your well-being but also that of your loved ones. But you have the power to change this.

Setting up safeguards is essential, especially when you're considering selling your business. Often, the success of a sale and the value you receive can hinge on the business's performance in the years following the transition. It's not only about keeping your business running smoothly, but also about attempting to maintain a valuable asset for potential buyers.

This brings us to eight critical protections you'll want to put in place. These steps are vital for maintaining security and stability for both your business and your family, giving you peace of mind as you move forward with your exit plans.

1. UMBRELLA INSURANCE

Let's talk about something that's a no-brainer for protecting yourself as a business owner, yet it's often overlooked: umbrella insurance. Think of it as an affordable safety net that goes above and beyond your standard insurance policies. It's number one on our list for a good reason.

Why is it so important? Well, in the business world, unexpected things happen. Say someone gets hurt at your business, or there's a car accident involving your company vehicle. If the costs of these incidents exceed what your regular insurance covers, umbrella insurance jumps in. It's like an extra layer of protection that kicks in when your other policies hit their limit.

And here's the best part: It's surprisingly inexpensive, especially considering the peace of mind it offers. As a business owner, you've got a lot on your plate, and the last thing you need is a lawsuit wiping out all your hard work. That's where umbrella insurance becomes a smart move. It protects not just your business but your personal assets, too. After all, you don't want a mishap in one part of your life to spill over and impact everything you've built.

So, think of umbrella insurance as your financial safety net. It's there to catch you when those unexpected, high-cost situations happen without breaking the bank. That's why I always recommend it as a top priority for business owners like you.

Whoever takes care of your automobile insurance can help you with umbrella insurance, or if you've already elected coverage, can help you review your limits. It's not uncommon for small business owners to carry several million dollars of umbrella coverage.

2. LIFE INSURANCE

Here's something that might sound obvious, but it's surprising how often it's overlooked: If you suddenly find yourself with angel wings, your business and family are going to be in a tight spot without you. It's a simple truth, yet I've seen many entrepreneurs, even those running multi-million-dollar businesses, act like they're immortal. They haven't paused to think about the "what ifs" of life—like illness or an unexpected accident—and as a result, they've neglected something as fundamental as life insurance.

Consider this: If you, the driving force behind your business, were no longer around, imagine the impact on your business's value and, by extension, your family's financial well-being. The most straightforward fix? Term life insurance. Let's say your business is valued at

$20 million. A term policy for that amount might cost you several thousand dollars annually. That's a small price for big peace of mind, especially if your business is the main income source for your family.

You don't need anything fancy—just something to bridge the gap between today and the sale. Many carriers offer a ten-year product with monthly premiums. The cost will depend on factors like your age, health, the policy's term, and its value. If you're a marathon runner, the premiums will likely be lower. If you're managing a health condition like Type II diabetes, it'll likely be much higher, but it's still a smart move for the security of your loved ones. You can always stop paying the premiums once you sell.

Once you have life insurance, remember to reassess your coverage regularly, especially if your business is growing. You want your coverage to increase as your company's value increases.

The idea here is to ensure your family isn't left out in the cold if you're no longer there. Think back to the "exit number" we discussed earlier—the ideal amount you want to net from selling your business. That number is a solid benchmark for setting your life insurance death benefit. For example, if you're aiming for a $15 million post-tax/fees exit, match it with a $15 million life insurance policy. It's a cost-effective way to tackle a significant risk. And the cherry on top? The death benefit is typically tax-free for the beneficiary.

3. BUSINESS SUCCESSION PLAN

For pre-exit entrepreneurs, the thought of leaving the business they've painstakingly built may seem distant, yet planning for this inevitability is crucial. This is where a succession plan comes into play, serving as a roadmap for the future of your business beyond your direct involvement.

The importance of a succession plan cannot be overstated. First and foremost, it provides clarity and direction for the future. Imagine if an unforeseen event, such as an illness or accident, abruptly takes you out of your leadership role. Without a clear successor or plan in place, your business could face significant challenges, from operational disruptions to potential conflicts among team members or family. A well-crafted succession plan addresses these concerns, outlining a clear transition of leadership and management to maintain stability.

Moreover, a succession plan is a signal to your employees, customers, and investors that the business is prepared for long-term sustainability. It demonstrates foresight and responsibility, helping the business you built continue to thrive, regardless of leadership changes. This can be especially reassuring to employees, who gain confidence in their job security and the future of the company.

For family-owned businesses, succession planning also involves delicate considerations around family dynamics and equitable treatment of heirs. It's about balancing family interests with the health of the business, ensuring that the next generation of leaders is prepared and capable.

Finally, as you approach the potential sale of your business, a solid succession plan can be a valuable asset. It shows prospective buyers that the business isn't reliant on any one person, making it a more attractive and sustainable investment.

In essence, a succession plan for a pre-exit entrepreneur isn't just about the end of a chapter; it's about writing the next one.

4. ESTATE PLAN

Understanding estate planning is crucial, and it's helpful to think of it in two stages: the 1.0 Estate Plan and the 2.0 Estate Plan. The 1.0 plan lays the foundational elements, while the 2.0 plan dives into more complex aspects like tax planning, aiming to minimize unnecessary taxes and maximize what you keep.

THE 1.0 ESTATE PLAN TYPICALLY INCLUDES:

1. **A will or trust:** This is the cornerstone of estate planning, outlining how your assets should be handled after your death

2. **Durable power of attorney:** This appoints someone to manage your financial affairs if you're unable to do so while you're alive.

3. **Medical/healthcare power of attorney:** Similarly, this designates someone to make medical decisions on your behalf if you're incapacitated.

4. **Advance directive:** This document specifies your wishes regarding end-of-life medical treatment if you can't communicate them yourself.
5. **Proper beneficiary designations:** These ensure that assets like life insurance policies and retirement accounts go to the people you've chosen.

Now, let's focus on **wills and trusts**, as they're key to estate planning.

A will provides instructions for distributing your assets after death. However, assets without a beneficiary designation typically go through probate—a public and sometimes lengthy legal process where your assets are retitled, and potential creditors may stake claims.

That's where a **trust** offers advantages. By setting up a trust, you can title significant assets like your home or brokerage account in the trust's name. You can also make the trust a beneficiary of certain assets. When you pass away, assets already in the trust or designated to it are distributed according to the trust's terms, bypassing the probate process. This not only maintains privacy but also works to provide a smoother transfer of your estate.

Essentially, it boils down to who you want to make decisions about your assets: you or the state. By proactively setting up your estate through a will or trust, you retain control over how your assets are distributed, to whom, and when.

The other documents above (2-5) are included with most planning fees when doing a will or trust with a trust and estate attorney.

THE 2.0 ESTATE PLAN

The 2.0 Estate Plan is where things get more nuanced. This stage involves sophisticated strategies for tax planning and wealth preservation. It's not just about who inherits your assets but also about how you can pass them on in the most tax-efficient way possible. This stage often involves working closely with someone like me, tax experts, and estate attorneys to navigate complex tax laws and find optimal solutions for your unique situation.

For instance, if you have a substantial estate, you might consider strategies like setting up charitable trusts or making planned gifts to reduce your taxable estate. Another approach could be to use life insurance policies in a way that benefits your heirs while minimizing tax liabilities. These strategies are tailored to not only preserve your wealth but also to align with your personal values and legacy goals.

It's important to remember that estate planning is not a "set it and forget it" task. It requires regular review and updates, especially as your financial situation evolves and tax laws change. Life events such as marriage, the birth of children or grandchildren, and even changes in your business can all necessitate adjustments to your estate plan.

Ultimately, both the 1.0 and 2.0 Estate Plans are about taking control of your financial legacy. They ensure that your hard-earned assets are distributed according to your wishes, providing peace of mind for you and your loved ones. By thoughtfully planning, you not only protect your assets but also craft a legacy that reflects your values and intentions.

5. DISABILITY INSURANCE

You're at the helm of your business, steering it toward success and growth. But have you considered how a sudden disability could affect your ability to lead and manage your company? This is where disability insurance becomes crucial. It's a safeguard which ensures that if you ever find yourself unable to work due to injury or illness, you won't have to worry about losing your income stream. For someone in your position, the financial implications of being out of work can be significant, not just for you but also for your business and employees.

Think of it as income protection. It helps maintain your financial stability and supports your family's lifestyle while you recover. It ensures that even if you face unexpected health challenges, your financial plans, including your exit strategy, remain on track. Moreover, it demonstrates to potential buyers and investors that the business has measures in place to mitigate risks associated with your unexpected absence, which could be a key factor in maintaining your company's value.

6. KEY PERSON INSURANCE

Key person insurance is a type of life insurance specifically designed to protect your business in the event that a crucial executive or team member passes away unexpectedly. To determine whether someone in your business qualifies as a "key person," consider the potential impact of their sudden absence. Ask yourself: Would their loss be catastrophic to your business operations? If the answer is yes, then key person insurance is a wise consideration for that individual.

Imagine, for instance, you run an engineering firm with an executive who is pivotal to a major project. This person's expertise and leadership are the driving force behind the project's success. If something happens to them, the project—and consequently your business—could face significant risks and financial upheaval. Key person insurance is designed to mitigate such risks. It provides the necessary funds to cope with the immediate financial challenges of finding and training a replacement, or to manage any other disruptions caused by the loss of that indispensable individual.

7. PERSONAL EMERGENCY FUNDS

Cash is more than just currency; it's a source of confidence. Ensuring you have sufficient cash reserves to comfortably cover your monthly expenses is key to maintaining your family's financial stability. The general rule of thumb varies depending on your income situation. If yours is a two-income household, aim to have around three months' worth of living expenses saved in cash. For one-income families, a minimum of six months' expenses is a prudent target. However, as an entrepreneur, you might find it wise to go beyond these standard guidelines, holding double or even triple these amounts. The goal is to have enough cash on hand to provide peace of mind and keep your confidence intact.

8. REGULAR CHECKUPS WITH YOUR WEALTH MANAGER

An essential aspect of your financial well-being is having someone who diligently monitors your risk management plan. This is where I come in. As your dedicated wealth manager, I don't just set up a plan and forget it; I conduct regular checkups to ensure that everything is on track and aligned with your changing needs and circumstances. My role is to keep a vigilant eye on various factors that could impact your financial health, continuously assessing and adjusting your plan to mitigate risks and capitalize on opportunities. This proactive approach is crucial in safeguarding what you've worked so hard to build.

For reasons I'll go into later in this book, I think it's a wise choice to have a wealth manager who is a CERTIFIED FINANCIAL PLANNER™ professional. A CFP® doesn't just focus on the investments they manage; they look at the bigger picture. This comprehensive view is vital because your financial life is more than just your investment portfolio. It encompasses insurance, estate planning, tax strategies, and more. Without a holistic approach, significant risks and opportunities could be overlooked. It's their responsibility to ensure that every aspect of your financial world is considered and that all parts of your financial life are working together harmoniously.

ACTION ITEMS

1. Review the eight key protections listed in this chapter. Which ones do you currently have in place? Which ones are you missing?

2. Set up a meeting with your wealth manager in the next thirty days. If you don't have a wealth manager or are unsure if yours is a good fit, I'd be glad to talk (my calendar: Goldfin.Group/Meeting). Make a plan to review this list and put the missing protections in place.

CHAPTER SIX

BUILDING YOUR TEAM OF A-PLAYERS

No matter how brilliant your mind or strategy, if you're playing a solo game, you'll always lose out to a team.

~Reid Hoffman

In the sale of your business, there's your team and the opposing team. And if you're selling to private equity, the opposing team went to Harvard for their MBAs and were eating their Wheaties as they landed in your town on their private jet.

I want you to have the best possible chance at success. There's no such thing as a *perfect* exit because, in the end, you are the one who determines what *perfect* means. There is no standardized metric to grade an exit.

That said, there are things you can do well ahead of time to help your exit be as smooth as the landing of the Gulfstream G700 carrying your company's buyers.

Let's get you a winning team, shall we?

A TEAM TO HELP YOU STICK THE LANDING

Picture your business exit like an Olympic gymnast's performance. Years of preparation lead to that one pivotal routine where every move counts. Just as a gymnast has a team of coaches, trainers, and specialists to perfect their routine and stick the landing, you need a team of expert advisors for your business exit. These professionals each contribute their expertise to help your exit be as rewarding as an Olympic gold-winning performance.

In this chapter, we'll identify the key members of your exit team, outlining the crucial role each plays in achieving your ultimate goal: a successful and profitable business transition.

1. WEALTH MANAGER (THAT'S ME)

In the financial world, many professionals can choose to label themselves as wealth managers. (There's nothing stopping anyone from using this title.) However, according to the CERTIFIED FINANCIAL PLANNER™ Board of Standards, in their December 2023 article, "CFP® Certification At 50: What's Next For Financial Planning?" only about one in three wealth managers carry the CERTIFIED FINANCIAL PLANNER™ certification. The CFP® is akin to a master's degree in personal finance, distinguishing those who have committed to a higher level of education and ethical standards. Unlike many "weekend" certifications available in the industry, achieving a CFP® requires a clean background and regulatory record, adherence to stringent ethical standards, ongoing continuing education, and passing a horrific comprehensive exam. This ensures that as your wealth manager, I am not only well-versed in the complexities of personal finance but also dedicated to acting in your best interests at all times.

On top of that, a *great* wealth manager is much more than a financial advisor; they're a pivotal part of your journey, especially during critical moments like a business exit. Acting as the quarterback of your exit team, they coordinate with professionals such as attorneys, accountants, and investment bankers, ensuring all the members of the team are rowing in the same direction. Their role is to simplify complex information and provide actionable advice, making the exit process efficient and effective, saving you time and money.

At the core of their service is behavioral coaching. They guide you through the emotional aspects of financial decision-making, helping you stay focused on long-term goals and avoid reactive decisions during market fluctuations. This is key to maintaining a disciplined investment approach.

Their role also involves comprehensive financial planning, covering everything from cashflow and estate planning to tax strategies and insurance. It's about creating a unified strategy that addresses all financial aspects of your life, ensuring harmony among various financial components.

Personalization is crucial. Your wealth manager tailors their advice to your unique situation and goals, providing customized strategies. They also educate you about investing principles and financial trends, empowering you to make informed decisions.

Often, when people think of a wealth manager, they primarily envision someone who manages their investment portfolio. While this is a part of what a wealth manager does, it's important to understand that portfolio management is actually one of the least critical components of their role and, arguably, the most commoditized. In today's world, numerous services and technologies automate a portfolio. What sets a great wealth manager apart, however, is not just their ability to oversee your investments, but their expertise in the broader aspects of financial planning (i.e., how the investments fit into your plan). They excel in areas that algorithms and automated services can't replicate—like providing personalized financial advice, understanding complex tax implications, and offering tailored strategies based on your unique life situation. In essence, while managing your portfolio is a service a wealth manager provides, it's their comprehensive approach and personalized guidance that truly add value to your financial journey.

In summary, a great wealth manager blends the roles of mentor, educator, strategist, and coach. They provide holistic guidance that goes beyond just managing assets, helping you navigate the complexities of personal finance with confidence and clarity.

2. TAX ADVISOR AND ACCOUNTANT

As you approach your business exit, the role of a tax advisor or accountant becomes increasingly pivotal. They're crucial in clarifying the tax implications of your sale, which can vary significantly from state to state. In fact, it's common for business owners to consider relocating to a more tax-friendly state, ideally six months prior to their sale, to optimize tax outcomes. Your accountant will be instrumental in preparing your business's financial statements for potential buyers, ensuring accuracy and transparency. This is a critical part of the due diligence process and the quality of the earnings report. If you're currently managing your own financials, like using QuickBooks, this might be the time to engage a professional tax firm. They can handle your books more efficiently and provide valuable tax advice. Many Certified Public Accountant (CPA) firms can offer audited financial statements, which have been reviewed by their peers. This is a valuable asset during the sale's due diligence phase. Such statements add credibility to your financial disclosures and can smooth the negotiation process.

Enlisting a top-tier accountant gives you the advantage of delegating complex and time-consuming financial tasks, especially during the demanding due diligence period. Their expertise not only helps with accuracy and compliance but also frees you up to focus on other critical aspects of your exit strategy, providing much-needed relief during this crucial phase.

3. BUSINESS BROKER OR M&A ADVISOR

An investment banker or business broker is pivotal in orchestrating the sale of your business. Their expertise lies not just in marketing your business effectively but also in managing the complex dynamics of the transaction. They start by preparing compelling marketing materials, such as teasers and Confidential Information Memorandums (CIMs), which are essential tools for attracting potential buyers. These documents are crafted to highlight the key aspects of your business, showcasing its value and potential in a professional and enticing manner.

Beyond marketing, these professionals play a critical role in keeping emotions in check throughout the sale process. Selling a business can be an emotionally charged experience, and having a seasoned banker or broker helps to mitigate emotional decision-making by employing a more strategic approach.

They also bring their extensive network of potential buyers to the table, opening doors to a range of interested parties. This network is invaluable in finding the right buyer who not only meets the financial criteria but also aligns with the future vision of your business.

Their involvement is key in securing a successful and profitable transaction, smoothing out the complexities, and guiding you through each step of the sale.

4. BUSINESS ATTORNEY

When navigating the intricacies of a business transaction, particularly during an exit, the importance of having a specialized business attorney cannot be overstated. It's crucial to choose an attorney who focuses on business transactions as their primary practice rather than a generalist. This specialization ensures they are deeply familiar with the nuances and complexities specific to business sales. A specialized business attorney will have a wealth of experience in drafting, reviewing, and negotiating contracts, understanding the unique legal challenges of business exits, and ensuring compliance with relevant laws.

5. TRUST AND ESTATE ATTORNEY

The role of a trust and estate attorney in your business exit process is both strategic and comprehensive. They are key in ensuring that your estate planning—both your foundational (1.0) and advanced (2.0) plans—aligns seamlessly with your exit strategy. Initially, they focus on getting your 1.0 Estate Plan in order, which includes updating your will or trust, and ensuring that all legal documents reflect your current wishes and circumstances. This foundational work is crucial as it lays the groundwork for a smooth transition of your assets and provides clear directives for their management.

As you move towards your exit, the attorney's role expands into the 2.0 plan, where they work closely with your financial team. This collaboration is vital for developing strategies to minimize the tax impact of your business sale. The attorney's expertise in estate law is crucial here, as they help navigate complex tax laws and explore various methods for tax-efficient asset transfer. By integrating these plans well ahead of your sale, the attorney helps to not only protect your legacy but also assists you in taking full advantage of legal opportunities to preserve your wealth.

6. INSURANCE ADVISOR

In the context of a business exit, an insurance advisor's role is centered on assessing and managing risk. They ensure that both your personal and business assets are adequately protected as you navigate the transition. This involves identifying potential risks that could arise during and after the sale process and recommending the appropriate insurance solutions to mitigate these risks.

The insurance advisor collaborates with other team members, such as your financial advisor and attorney, to align their strategies with the overall exit plan. They might suggest updating existing policies or acquiring new ones to cover any gaps in coverage. This could include key person insurance, liability insurance, or even a personal umbrella policy. Their expertise in insurance provides a safety net that safeguards the financial gains from your business exit in an attempt to ensure a secure future for you and your family.

7. BUSINESS COACH OR CONSULTANT

In the journey of preparing for a business exit, the guidance of a business coach can be transformative, particularly one skilled in the Entrepreneurial Operating System (EOS). This is a comprehensive business system that provides a set of simple, practical tools to help entrepreneurs and their leadership teams improve the operational value of their businesses. A coach proficient in EOS can help you apply these principles to create a more streamlined, efficient, and potentially more valuable business as you approach your exit.

Working with an EOS coach involves diving deep into the six key components of your business: Vision, People, Data, Issues, Process, and Traction. This system encourages a holistic approach to business management, ensuring that all aspects of your company are aligned and working efficiently towards a common goal. With their expertise, an EOS coach can guide you in refining your business vision, getting the right people in the right seats, making data-driven decisions, resolving issues effectively, systemizing your business processes, and gaining traction to achieve your vision. This level of professional coaching is invaluable as it not only prepares your business for a successful exit but also enhances its overall marketability and appeal to potential buyers.

8. EXECUTIVE COACH

An executive coach is invaluable in guiding you through the emotional landscape of selling your business. This is more than just a financial transition; it's a significant shift in your life. As a driven business owner, you'll likely experience a range of emotions during this process. A skilled coach can provide support and perspective, helping you navigate these feelings effectively as you move towards your exit.

9. HUMAN RESOURCES ADVISOR

In a business exit, an HR advisor plays a vital role, especially when your workforce is a key asset. They expertly handle the transition of employees, shaping communication strategies, and ensuring that employee-related aspects are seamlessly integrated into the sale process. Their involvement is critical in managing due diligence, assessing cultural fit for potential integration, and negotiating employee-related terms. By effectively handling these human capital elements, an HR advisor not only helps maintain employee morale and retain key talent but also positively influences the overall valuation of your business, making them an invaluable member of your exit team.

10. NETWORK, FORUM, OR MASTERMIND

Your network, forum, or mastermind group serves as a vital support system during the significant transition of a business exit. Whether it's a close-knit mastermind, a professional network, or an intimate forum, this group provides invaluable support. Here, you can share experiences and gain insights with peers who understand the challenges that come with running and exiting a business. The collective wisdom of those who have already navigated similar paths can be a source of comfort and guidance during what can be a stressful time. Their experiences and advice can provide practical and emotional support, helping you navigate your journey with confidence and a sense of shared understanding. I cannot overstate the importance of having a group of peers with similar problems. As humans, we bond over shared experiences, and because business owners are a minority by far, we need a group to "do life with" who are in a similar situation to us.

A TEAM OF A-PLAYERS

As we've discussed throughout this chapter, surrounding yourself with a team of A-players is non-negotiable for a successful business exit. These professionals should be seasoned experts with experience in guiding entrepreneurs through exits. While it's in an entrepreneur's nature to tackle challenges head-on, your business exit is not the time for do-it-yourself approaches or on-the-job training for your advisors. This is a pivotal moment, marking the culmination of years of dedication. Be sure you're backed by a team of skilled professionals who bring both experience and professionalism to the table. As you move forward with confidence, rest assured that you are in capable hands, setting the stage for a successful transition. In the final chapter, we'll conclude our journey with key takeaways and steps on how we can collaborate effectively to make your exit as smooth and rewarding as possible.

ACTION ITEMS

1. Who advises you now in each of these areas, and why did you choose them? Who else do you need to add to your A-Players?
   - Wealth
   - Tax
   - Selling the Business
   - Business Law
   - Trust and Estate
   - Property and Casualty Insurance and Life Insurance
   - Business Coaching/Consulting
   - Executive Coaching
   - Human Resources

2. Once you've listed the who and why, determine if they're a good member of your exit team.

3. Where are your people, and how often do you see them?
   - If you're not part of a group, go date a few.
   - Most entrepreneurs' groups will allow you to come as a guest. Check out Entrepreneurs' Organization (EO) and C12 (if you're a kingdom-minded Christian).

CHAPTER SEVEN

GRANTING YOURSELF PERMISSION TO EXIT

The man who moves a mountain begins by carrying away small stones.

~Confucius

We've covered a lot of ground in this brief book.

We've talked about a number of key areas to consider when it comes to your business exit: your family and values, your goals and personal interests, your overall financial picture, and why you must think long-term, about your protection, and your team and process.

I've given you quite a bit to think about. But before we wrap up, I want to leave you with the core message of the book, so you don't miss the forest for the trees. I also want to give you a few next steps to consider.

When it comes to the sale of your company, you want to make the smartest play. But as the offers start rolling in, it's natural to second-guess yourself. You'll begin asking questions like these:

- Will I be able to maintain my lifestyle?
- How much is really enough?
- Am I selling too soon?
- What am I going to do next?

It would be gut-wrenching to look back with regret. Why? Because it's not only about getting a fair valuation. It's also about setting your family up for lifelong success and maintaining a sizable bucket for your next entrepreneurial pursuit.

Earlier in the book, I shared my experience with building and selling a business. I know what it's like to have most of your net worth tied up in your company, and how tempting it can be when the first offers start hitting your desk.

It's a lot to process, which is why you need an expert who has the right experience and credentials.

HOW I CAN HELP

In your business exit journey, I serve not just as an advisor but as a long-term partner, understanding your unique needs both pre-and-post-exit. This partnership is crucial because it's about more than just transactions; it's about understanding your goals and values across different life stages and business endeavors.

In wealth management, we intersect your personal aspirations with your financial resources, blending the quantitative aspects of capital (the math and the data) with the qualitative facets of your life's ambitions (what makes you—you).

As your wealth manager, consider me like a primary care physician who not only refers you to specialists but also accompanies you to every appointment, ensuring a cohesive treatment plan.

This role extends beyond traditional wealth planning; it's about forming a deep understanding of what matters to you, guiding you through various life transitions, and being there for both the dollars-and-cents decisions and the more emotional, abstract aspects of your financial life.

It's a partnership where I bring my experience and insights to bear on every aspect of your journey, from the intricate details of your business exit to the broader picture of your personal and financial future.

LET'S TALK

You might wonder what it's like to work with Goldfin Group as you consider your exit.

As you can imagine, wealth managers will knock down your door after you sell, but that's not our style. My team and I treat you like you're liquid…before you're liquid. It's the only way we can help you plan for your most advantageous deal—one that goes beyond money, and accounts for everything else that matters just as much.

It's worth a confidential conversation. Here's how to get started.

1. Grab a time to chat. Visit us online to schedule a short intro call at <u>Goldfin.Group/Meeting</u>.
2. Go a little deeper. If we mutually decide to continue our initial conversation, we'll schedule time for you to share more about your circumstances and goals.
3. Get your number. By the third time we talk, you'll get a recommended number and path to secure it.

At no point in these three calls will you commit to our services. In fact, even as our client, there are no contract periods. Your money is your money.

I'd be honored to have a conversation.

THE GOLDFIN MOMENT

Even if, after you've read the book and worked through the action steps outlined at the end of each chapter, you're still feeling hesitant, that's completely natural.

Don't let that keep you from what I call the "Goldfin Moment." It's the moment when the money is finally in the bank, and you're officially free to go after whatever is calling you next.

Granting yourself *permission to exit* is the first vital step in this transformative process. It's about acknowledging that you are ready for what's next and equipped with the knowledge, planning, and expert support to make your transition successful. As your financial guide, I am committed to accompanying you on this journey, ensuring that when you grant yourself permission to exit, it's with certainty and readiness for the exciting opportunities that await.

For more insight, information,
and inspiration, listen to the

NOTHING BUT NEXT PODCAST

APPENDIX

GOLDFIN GROUP SERVICES

EXIT STRATEGY
- Determining the number to achieve financial freedom
- Timing guidance: when to sell for optimal value
- Emotional readiness evaluation
- Evaluation and prepping of your exit team
- Key employee retention
- Vetting potential successors or buyers

ENTREPRENEURIAL DECISIONS
- Guided self-assessment
- Leadership retreats (Goldfin Summit)
- Strategic planning and vision setting
- Navigating the emotional side of selling

HOLISTIC FINANCIAL HEALTH
- Investment Planning
- Portfolio Management
- Cashflow planning
- Goals-based planning
- Insurance adequacy
- Estate planning strategies
- Tax planning strategies
- Debt management and optimization
- Liquidity planning

PERSONAL GROWTH AND DEVELOPMENT
- Work-life balance strategies
- Guidance on post-exit role transitions
- Encouraging life in accordance with personal values and principles

BUSINESS HEALTH AND GROWTH
- Identifying potential weak links in the business

PLEASE REVIEW THIS BOOK

If you enjoyed this book, would you take a few moments to leave a review wherever you purchased it (and perhaps even Goodreads.com)? I'm grateful for your support. Thank you!

GRATITUDE

Dad, thank you for being my buddy. We have our moments, as any father and son do, but I know I'm blessed to have you in my life. When you say you're excited for me, I believe you. When I need support, you always have advice racked and in the chamber. Thank you.

Mom, your ability to engage a community has always been an inspiration, but I didn't realize how great you are at it until I saw it year-over-year in my thirties. I pray it's genetic and that this book can engage a community to think more clearly about their purpose in life! I also love to write because of you. Thank you for loving your son despite his flaws.

Amanda, my beautiful wife, and mother to my boys. Thank you for blessing my life's missions by holding down the fort, encouraging me, talking with me, showing me God's grace (a lot), and always reminding me of what's most important. I love you like crazy.

To the boys, you keep me young and give me life. You give me a reason to work to be the best I can be every day. Success takes hard work and determination, but you must have fun along the way. I'll always love you. P.S. Did I ever tell you how lucky you are?

To Cat, you've been my right hand for the past six years, and I wouldn't have it any other way. We make a great team. Thank you for serving our clients the way you do—with the utmost respect and diligence. You're a pro!

~ Ryan Guth, December 2023

WHO IS RYAN GUTH?

Ryan Guth leads Goldfin Group from Nashville, TN, where he combines strategic financial guidance with a deep understanding of entrepreneurs' pivotal transitions. His leadership reflects a blend of professional insight and personal commitment, guiding clients toward aligning their financial strategies with their God-given purpose and gifts. Ryan is a CERTIFIED FINANCIAL PLANNER™ professional. He is married to his wife, Amanda, and is the father to three boys.

Certified Financial Planner Board of Standards Center for Financial Planning, Inc. owns and licenses the certification marks CFP®, CERTIFIED FINANCIAL PLANNER™, and CFP® (with plaque design) in the United States to Certified Financial Planner Board of Standards, Inc., which authorizes individuals who successfully complete the organization's initial and ongoing certification requirements to use the certification marks.

Printed in the USA
CPSIA information can be obtained
at www.ICGtesting.com
JSHW071256100324
58840JS00006B/15